BLS WORKING PAPERS

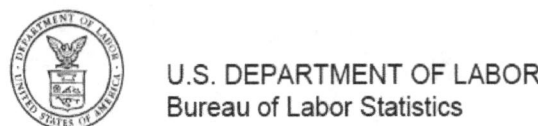 U.S. DEPARTMENT OF LABOR
Bureau of Labor Statistics

OFFICE OF EMPLOYMENT AND UNEMPLOYMENT
STATISTICS

Recent Trends in Job Stability and Job Security: Evidence from the March CPS

Jay Stewart, U.S. Bureau of Labor Statistics

Working Paper 356
March 2002

February 25, 2002

Recent Trends in Job Stability and Job Security:
Evidence from the March CPS

Jay Stewart
Office of Employment Research
        and Program Development
Bureau of Labor Statistics
2 Massachusetts Avenue, NE
Room 4945
Voice (202) 691-7376
FAX   (202) 691-7425
E-Mail Stewart_J@bls.gov

* I thank Dave Jaeger, Maury Gittleman, Mike Pergamit, Anne Polivka, Jim Spletzer, and Ken Swinnerton for comments and suggestions on earlier versions of this paper. Any opinions expressed here are mine, and do not necessarily reflect those of the Bureau of Labor Statistics.

Recent Trends in Job Stability and Job Security

Abstract

Over the past few years there has been a keen interest, both in the popular press and among researchers, in whether job stability and job security have declined. Anecdotal evidence suggests that stability and security declined in the 1980s and 1990s. But academic studies have been divided in their findings. This paper uses sheds additional light on this question using data from the March CPS. The main advantage to using March CPS data is that the transition variables are defined consistently over the 1975-76 through 2000-2001 period covered by my data. I find that overall job separation rates changed very little over this time period, but that there were large changes in the component transitions. Employment-to-unemployment transitions declined dramatically, indicating a significant increase in job security. For men, nearly all of the increase in job security occurred in the 1990s, while for women, the increase was more uniform throughout the period. There was an equally dramatic increase in employment-to-employment transitions (job changes with two or fewer weeks of unemployment), indicating that it has become easier to change employers. I also examine trends in these transitions treating married couples as a unit. I find that job stability fell for married couples, but that job security increased. The decrease in stability would have been smaller and the increase in security would have been larger were it not for the increase in the proportion of couples in which the wife's earnings are a significant share of total earnings.

I. Introduction

Over the past few years, there has been a keen interest, both in the popular press and among researchers, in whether job stability and job security have declined in recent years.[1] With the recession that began in early 2001, there will be a renewed interest in this issue. Changes in job security have obvious implications for the welfare of workers. It is well known that job losers spend more time unemployed, and that they suffer persistent earnings losses after they find new jobs.[2] However, it is less obvious why we should care about job stability. A decline in job stability could be either good news or bad news for workers, depending on the reason for the decline. For example, job stability could decline because economic conditions have worsened and workers have become more likely to lose jobs. Or stability could decline because economic conditions have improved and workers are finding better jobs.

One reason stable jobs are desirable from a policy perspective is that often a large portion of workers' retirement benefits are tied to their jobs. It is well known that workers with defined benefit plans receive substantially lower benefits if they change jobs frequently. However, job changing could result in lower retirement benefits for workers in 401(k) plans if they cash out their accounts when they separate from their employers. A study by Employee Benefit Research Institute (Yakoboski 1997) shows that in 1996, 60 percent of job changers cashed out their 401(k) balances rather than rolling them over into a qualified plan or an IRA. Most of these

---

[1] *Job stability* refers to the duration of jobs, without regard to the reasons for increasing or decreasing duration. Examples of job stability measures used in the literature include retention rates (Swinnerton and Wial 1995,1996, Marcotte 1996, and Diebold, Neumark, and Polsky 1996,1997, and Neumark, Polsky, and Hansen 1999), job tenure (Farber 1998), the fraction of workers in new jobs (Jaeger and Stevens 1999), and turnover (Rose 1995, and Monks and Pizer 1998). *Job security* refers to the extent to which job separations are involuntary. The primary measure of job security is the rate of job loss (Polsky 1999, Farber 1997a,c, Boisjoly, Duncan, and Smeeding 1998, Monks and Pizer 1998, and Valletta 1999) and the employment-to-unemployment transition rate (Stewart 2000).
[2] See Ruhm (1991).

were younger workers cashing out relatively small balances. However, as noted by Yakoboski (1997), "It can be argued from a financial planning perspective that even relatively small sums can compound into nontrivial contributions to a retirement nest egg over a period of decades. Furthermore, the importance of preservation of seemingly small balances is enhanced by the fact that individuals may receive a number of these 'small' distributions over the course of a career."

In this paper, I use transition data constructed from the 1976-2001 March Current Population Survey (CPS) to examine trends in job stability from January 1975 through March 2001. The March CPS data have several advantages over other commonly used datasets. The transition variables are consistently defined from the 1975-76 period through the 2000-2001 period, which permits me to look at trends over a longer period of time and to look at recent trends. The large sample size of the March CPS makes it possible to identify changes for specific demographic groups. The CPS collects information about everybody in the household, so it is possible to examine trends for married couples. Although the March CPS data do not have information on the reason for a separations, it is possible to classify separations into component transitions that roughly correspond to the three gross flows transitions out of employment (employment to employment, employment to unemployment, and employment to not in labor force).

Extending the analysis to married couples is a significant addition to the literature, because of the increased importance of wives' earnings to family income. The fraction of married women who worked any time during the year increased from 53 percent on 1975 to 64 percent in 2000. (The March employment-to-population ratio of married women increased from 43 percent in 1976 to 60 percent in 2001.) This greater labor force participation has led to an increase in wives' contributions to the earnings of married couples. In 1975, the wife earned 23 percent of the average couple's total weekly earnings.[3] By 2000, the wife's share had increased to 34 percent. The fraction of couples that rely on the wife's earnings for a significant portion of earnings also increased. In 1975, men were the primary earners (i.e., earned more than 60 percent of the couple's income) in 77 percent of married couples, while women were the primary earners in 6 percent of couples. The remaining 17 percent were equal-earner couples (i.e., couples in which both spouses earned 40 or more percent of the couple's total earnings). By 2000, men were the primary earners in only 58 percent of married couples, while women were primary earners in 12 percent. Equal-earner couples increased to 29 percent of all couples.

Ironically, the increased prevalence of equal-earner couples could have worked in the direction of decreasing job stability and security. For equal-earner couples, the loss of either job will result in a significant loss of income. In contrast, for primary-earner couples, a significant loss of income occurs only if the primary earner loses his or her job. This implies that it is far more likely that an equal-earner couple will experience a significant loss of income due to a job loss. To illustrate, suppose that the chance of job loss is 5 percent in all jobs, and that husbands' and wives' job loss probabilities are not correlated. A primary-earner couple has a 5 percent chance of a significant loss of income, while the equal-earner couple faces nearly a 10 percent chance of a significant loss of income.

---

[3] This average includes women who did not work for pay.

II. Background and Previous Research

The popular perception is that jobs were both less stable and less secure in the 1980s than in the 1970s and that this decline in stability and security continued into the 1990s.[4] However, the evidence from academic studies has been mixed.

Studies that have looked at job stability generally fall into two groups. Studies that used data from the Panel Study of Income Dynamics (PSID) have found that job stability has decreased (Rose 1995 and Marcotte 1996), while those that used data from the Current Population Survey (CPS) Tenure Supplements have found little or no change in job stability (Swinnerton and Wial 1995,1996, Farber 1998, and Diebold, Neumark, and Polsky 1997).[5] Diebold, Neumark, and Polsky (1997) show that much of the decrease in job stability found in the PSID can be traced to a change in the questions used to determine turnover. Even so, the CPS tenure supplement is not without its problems. The main tenure question changed in 1983, although it is less obvious how serious this break in series is. Given the difference in findings by data source, much of the debate has centered on data issues and how to adjust for breaks in series, most importantly how to handle breaks in series in both the CPS Tenure Supplement data and the PSID.[6] Jaeger and Stevens (1999) took the natural step of comparing measures from these two datasets. The found that there has been no change in the incidence of short duration jobs,[7] and, more importantly, they found no difference between the two datasets.

Several more recent papers (Gottschalk and Moffitt 1999, Bansak and Raphael 1998, and Fitzgerald 1999) have used SIPP data and found no change in job stability between the early

---

[4] See Neumark and Polsky (1998).

[5] Gottschalk and Moffitt (1994) make this point. It is worth noting that the studies using PSID data exclude women.

[6] See Stewart (1998) for a detailed discussion of the data issues in the job stability literature.

[7] Gottschalk and Moffitt (1999) also find no change in job stability using PSID data.

1980s and the early 1990s. The advantage of the SIPP data is that the measure of job stability is consistently defined in all years. But the data span only 10 years--from the early 1980s through the early 1990s. Hence, it is not possible to use SIPP data to compare the 1970s to the 1980s and later years, or to look a recent trends in job stability.

Because the primary measure of job security is the job-loss rate, most researchers looking at this question have used either the Current Population Survey (CPS) Displaced Worker Supplements (DWS), the Panel Study of Income Dynamics (PSID), or the National Longitudinal Surveys (NLS). Studies by Boisjoly, Duncan, and Smeeding (1998), Monks and Pizer (1998), Polsky (1999), and Valletta (1999) have found that job loss appears to have been more common in the late 1980s and early 1990s than in the 1970s. Polsky (1999) also found that the consequences (lost earnings and likelihood of unemployment) have become more severe. But as in the job stability debate, data quality is an important issue.[8] All of these datasets have, in principle, the correct measure, but they also have breaks in series that make it difficult to generate a consistent series over a long period (and sometimes even a short period) of time. Although researchers have devised clever ways to adjust for these breaks in series, one can never be sure whether observed changes are real or due to changes in the survey instruments.

Only two other studies that I am aware of look at trends in job stability and job security past the early 1990s. Neumark, Polsky, and Hansen (1999) extends Diebold, Neumark, and Polsky (1997) to include 4-year retention rates between 1991 and 1995. Farber (1997c, 2001) extends an earlier paper (Farber 1997a) to include data from the 1996 and 2000 DWS.

Even over a period of time as short as the 1990s, these authors have had to address breaks in series. In the study by Neumark, Polsky, and Hansen (1999), the break came about because

---

[8] See Stewart (2000) for a discussion of the data issues in the job security literature.

there was no Tenure Supplement in 1995. So in order to compute 4-year retention rates they used tenure data from the 1995 CPS Contingent Worker Supplement, which asks different tenure questions than the Tenure Supplements. After adjusting the data to account for the difference in questions Neumark, Polsky, and Hansen found no change in overall job stability, although stability increased for low tenure workers and decreased for higher tenure workers. In the studies by Farber (1997c,2001), the break in series was caused by a subtle change in wording of the main question in the 1996 DWS. The 1996 question places greater emphasis on leaving a job than do the earlier questions. This wording change most likely is the reason for the large increase in the "Other" category (see Abraham 1997). Even ignoring the "Other" category, there was still no decline in the job-loss rate after the 1990-91 recession, suggesting that job security declined in the 1990s.

The present paper contributes to the literature by bringing a new data source to bear on the issues of job stability and security, by analyzing trends through the 1990s, and by extending the analysis to married couples.

III. Data

In this study, I use data from the March CPS files from 1976-2001. My sample consists of men and women age 19 and above in March[9] who worked at least one week in the previous year, and were between the ages of 18 and 54 in March of the previous year. Because I am interested in whether job stability has changed for workers in regular (post-schooling) jobs, I omit individuals with less than one year of potential experience.[10]   I also excluded self-

---

[9] I used 19 rather than 18 as the cutoff because the age refers to the age at the time of the survey.
[10] I use this restriction because it is not possible to identify students and recent graduates on a consistent basis over the years covered by my data.

employed workers[11] and people who worked less that 35 hours per week in the previous year. To simplify computation of standard errors and keep the dataset to a manageable size, I used only the first four rotation groups leaving me with a sample of 550,845 observations.[12]

To generate transition variables, I use information from both the Basic CPS and the Income Supplement. The Basic CPS contains information about the individual's labor force status during the reference week in March, while the Income Supplement contains information about what the individual was doing last year. Combining this information, it is possible to determine whether a worker separated from his or her employer during the 14 ½ months between January of the previous year and March of the current year, and what type of transition the worker experienced.

For my measure of job stability, I use the job separation rate. An upward trend in the job separation rate indicates a decline in job stability. Because changes in the separation rate can occur for many reasons, it is useful to classify separations into component transitions. Although the March CPS data do not allow me to identify separations as being voluntary or involuntary, it is possible to classify separations into three categories that roughly correspond to the gross flows transitions. These are: job changes that are accompanied by two or fewer weeks of unemployment (EE transitions),[13] employment-to-unemployment (EU) transitions (including job changes that were accompanied by 3+ weeks of unemployment), and employment-to-not-in-

---

[11] To insure that the sample is consistently defined over time, incorporated self-employed workers are included in the sample. Also, I included wage and salary workers who have some self-employment income.

[12] Using the full sample would result in a relatively small decline in standard errors. If the observations were independent there would be a 40 percent reduction in the standard errors. But because each individual shows up twice (in consecutive years) in the full sample, it would be necessary to account for the covariance between observations making the actual reduction much smaller.

[13] The two-or-fewer-weeks distinction was made because the weeks-unemployed-last-year question is not asked if the worker worked 50 or more weeks during the previous year.

labor-force (EN) transitions.[14] The EU transition rate is counter-cyclical (see Figures 1-3), which indicates that EU transitions are largely involuntary. Furthermore, Stewart (2000) has shown that nearly all of the variation in the EU transition rate is due to job loss.[15] For this reason, I use the EU transition rate as my measure of job security. The EE transition rate, in contrast, is pro-cyclical, which indicates that these are largely voluntary transitions. Finally, I would expect that the vast majority of EN transitions are voluntary, although they could include some workers who lost a job, became unemployed, and then left the labor force because they became discouraged.

Formal Definitions

An individual is considered to have separated from a job if he or she changed jobs or was not employed in during the reference week in March. To be classified as a job changer, the worker had to be employed during the reference week in March and meet at least one of the following conditions: (1) the worker had more than one employer in the previous year,[16] (2) the worker experienced more than one spell of unemployment in the previous year,[17] or (3) the

---

[14] Although the component transitions are similar to the gross flows transitions, there are a couple of important differences. First, the gross flows count the number of transitions, while I count the number of people who make the transition. For example, in the gross flows, someone who makes an EU transition, an UE transition, and another EU transition would be counted as having experienced two EU transitions. In my analysis, I count one person as having experienced an EU transition. This single counting is more appropriate, because I am interested in changes in the fraction of workers who experienced these transitions, not the total number of transitions. Second, my definition of an EE transition differs from the gross flows definition in that I only include workers who changed jobs. The gross flows definition also includes people who worked at the same employer in both months.

[15] Stewart's (2000) EU transition rate is slightly different in that he does not include job changes that were accompanied by 3+ weeks of unemployment.

[16] One concern is that the number-of-employers question might be picking up multiple jobholders. However, the question specifically states that concurrently held jobs are to be counted as one job. Further, the 1976-1987 Income Supplements asked whether the respondent looked for work between jobs, which gives interviewers another opportunity to make sure that the response to the number of employers question is correct. The looked-for-work question was not asked in 1988 and later years, but there was no jump in the average number of jobs held last year between 1987 and 1988. Hence, multiple jobholding does not a appear to be a problem.

[17] This criterion does not include workers with exactly one spell of unemployment, because one spell of unemployment does not imply a job change. It is impossible to tell whether the individual was initially unemployed

worker reported a change in 1-digit industry code between the longest job last year and the main job last week.[18,19]

Separations were classified into the three transitions as follows. Everybody who was unemployed or NILF in March of the current year is classified as an EU or EN transition, respectively. Individuals who changed jobs were divided into two groups: those whose job changes were accompanied by 3 or more weeks of unemployment, and those whose job changes were accompanied by 2 or fewer weeks of unemployment. Those with 3 or more weeks of unemployment were classified as EU transitions, while all other job changes were classified as EE transitions. Note that the numerator in these transition rates is not the number transitions, but the number of *workers* who experienced the transition at least once during the 14½ month period between January of the previous year and the reference week in March of the current year.

Changes in the CPS

---

and found a job or was initially employed and left a job. Of course, workers with only one spell of unemployment can still be classified as separations via (1) or (3).

By requiring at least two spells of unemployment, I implicitly assume that the worker held a job between the two spells. It is possible that the individual left the labor force between the spells of unemployment. A misclassification would occur only if the worker began the year unemployed and experienced the following transitions: unemployed to NILF, NILF to unemployed, and unemployed to working. To avoid this misclassification, I did not include individuals who reported that they worked in the same job in March, because these are likely to be temporary layoffs. Individuals were considered to be in the same job if the industry and occupation codes for longest job last year matched (at the three-digit level) the industry and occupation codes for the main job in March.

[18] The main reason for including this criterion is to detect job changes that occurred between December of the previous year and the reference week in March. This criterion also picks up separations that occurred in the previous year, but were not picked up by (1) because the person did not find a new job until the current year.

It is possible to use changes in the industry code to determine whether a job change occurred because industry and occupation are dependently coded. This means that the interviewer determines whether the respondent's job last year is the same as the job last week based on the verbatim descriptions of the two jobs and additional probes when necessary. If the jobs were the same, the interviewer marks a check item and the longest job last year was given the same industry and occupation codes as the main job last week. If not, the industry and occupation codes are collected as usual. The advantage of dependent coding is that it greatly reduces the number of spurious changes in industry and occupation codes.

An important issue in the job stability and job security literature is the comparability of data over time. While there have been no changes in the main questions used to determine turnover, there have been two changes in the CPS during the period covered by my data. Fortunately, both of these changes have been well documented, and there are data available from which I can derive adjustment factors. Below, I describe these breaks and my adjustments.

The first change occurred in 1989 when the Census Bureau overhauled the CPS processing system. There were many changes, but what is most relevant for my purposes is that Census changed the procedures used to impute missing data. Beginning in 1989, the Census changed the criteria by which variables were allocated, and it began imputing entire Income Supplement records using a hot deck procedure (I will refer to these observations as "FL-665 observations").[20]

There are several reasons why an entire record would be imputed. First, it may not have been possible to match the Income Supplement record to the Basic record for an individual in the household, even though other individuals were matched.[21] Second, it was not possible to match the Income Supplement record to the Basic record for anybody in the household. Finally, the entire record would be imputed if there were not enough data collected on the Income Supplement. Although allocating the entire record for these cases means that some collected

---

[19] The vast majority (81.1 percent) of all job changes were identified by the number-of-jobs condition. The remaining 18.9 percent were identified by unemployment spells condition (6.4 percent), and the industry-change condition (12.5 percent).

[20] Ideally, imputed values would be omitted from the sample. Unfortunately, it is not possible to identify imputed values for industry last year before 1989, and only some imputed values can be identified in 1989 and later years. Since I am looking at trends, it is more important that the data be as consistent as possible over time as possible. Hence, except for the FL-665 observations described below and in the Appendix, imputed values are included, even for years when they can be identified.

[21] This type of missing observation occurred because the Basic CPS and the Income Supplement were separate booklets. With the advent of computer assisted interviewing, these types of nonmatches were eliminated.

data are not used, it has the advantage of insuring that the data on a single record are internally consistent.

Overall, about 10 percent of the post-1988 sample is composed of FL-665 observations, with the second reason (no matches for anybody in the household) accounting for the lion's share--about 80 percent. Anecdotal evidence suggests that about half of these, about 40 percent of FL-665 observations, were allocated because the interviewer chose not to conduct the interview.[22] Therefore, up to 60 percent of FL-665 observations, or about 6 percent of the sample, are missing for reasons related to the respondent. Keep in mind that these observations still would have been allocated under the old processing system, but they would have been allocated using different procedures. Hence, my goal in adjusting the data is to make the pre-1989 data and the post-1988 data as comparable as possible. Because it is not possible to identify the observations that would have been FL-665 observations in the pre-1989 data, my adjustment tries to replicate the earlier processing system in the later data. So I omit all of the FL-665 observations from my sample, and make two adjustments to the remaining data.

Both of the adjustments are straightforward. The first adjustment reweights the data to account for the fact that the demographic composition of the FL-665 observations differs somewhat from that of the rest of the sample. For each year of the sample, I estimated the probability that an observation is a FL-665 observation based on demographic characteristics and labor force status from the Basic CPS. I then use these predicted probabilities to reweight the data so that observations that are more likely to be missing are given greater weight. This adjustment maintains the composition of the sample.

_____

[22] In the past there were not strong incentives to collect the supplement data. Interviewers' performance evaluations were based on completion of Basic CPS interviews, but not on supplements. To illustrate, when the Los Angeles

The second adjustment corrects for any within group differences in the probability of a transition that are attributable to the difference in processing systems. To make this adjustment it is necessary to have data that were processed under both the new and old processing systems. Fortunately, such data exist. The March 1988 CPS, which was the last data file to be processed under the old system, was reprocessed using the new system. For each type of transition, I computed the transition rate for each of 32 age/education/sex cells using the two versions of the March 1988 CPS data. For each cell and each transition, I computed the ratio of the transition rate from the data processed under the new and old systems. This yielded 32 adjustment factors for each of the 4 transitions I examine. Finally, I reweighted the microdata using these adjustment factors.

The second change occurred in 1994. In that year, the Basic CPS questionnaire was completely redesigned and computer assisted interviewing (CAI) was introduced. The March CPS was not redesigned, although it was converted to CAI. Most of the variables used to define separations come from the Income Supplement and, hence, were not affected by the redesign. The variable that is potentially affected is the Employment Status Recode (ESR [PEMLR in the redesigned CPS]).[23]

Research by Polivka and Miller (1998) provides some guidance on how to adjust the data. They found that the redesign had a small effect on the unemployment rate.[24] So I

---

field office increased the incentives to collect supplemental data, the number of missing supplements fell by about half.

[23] The industry and occupation sequence of questions changed as well. The primary difference is that they are now dependently coded from month to month. This does not affect criterion (3) for identifying job changers, because industry is still dependently coded between the main job last week and the longest job held last year.

[24] The effect on the unemployment rate was larger for people aged 55 and older. However, by restricting my analysis to people with 40 or fewer years of potential experience, there are very few of 55+ year-old workers in my sample.

reweighted the pre-1994 microdata using the adjustment factors in Polivka and Miller (1998) to make them comparable to the post-1993 data.[25]

IV. Trends in Job Stability and Job Security

Figures 1-3 summarize the trends of the four transitions for all workers, men, and women. Overall job stability did not change much over the 1975-2000 period, but there were sharp differences between men and women. The separation rate for all workers decreased slightly (from 25.0 percent to 22.9 percent), with the decline being larger for women (5.3 percentage points) than for men (0.7 percentage points). The slight decline in the overall separation rate masks significant changes in the component transitions. The EE transition rate increased by 5.1 percentage points (59 percent), while the EU transition rate fell by 5.0 percentage points (47 percent). The large decline in the EU transition rate indicates that job security increased significantly over this time period. We can also see that the larger decline in the separation rate for women is largely due to the dramatic decline the in their EN transition rate. This is consistent with the trend toward greater labor force participation among women, and it suggests that much of the increase in female employment is due to a lower exit rate from employment.

Table 1 shows the coefficients from probit equations estimated over the entire sample. All equations include a time trend variable as well as dummy variables to control for race (white/nonwhite), marital status, age (4 categories), education (4 categories), and region (4 categories). To simplify presentation, I have omitted the coefficients on the control variables. The top row of Table 1 contains coefficients on the time trend variable for each transition for all

_____

[25] The adjustment for other EU transitions accounts for that job changes that are accompanied by some

-13-

men and all women. Subsequent rows contain coefficients on the time trend variable interacted with age, education, and race variables. Separate equations were run for each group of variables, and all coefficients are expressed as marginal effects. Table 2 shows the change over the 1975-2000 period (calculated from the probit estimates) as a percentage of 1975 transition rates.

Results from probit equations confirm that, even after controlling for demographic changes, there have been only slight changes in the overall separation rate for men and women and significant changes in some of the component transitions. For both men and women, there was a large increase in the EE transition rate and a large decline in the EU transition rate. The EN transition rate decreased significantly for women, and remained roughly constant for men.

Looking at the lower portion of Tables 1 and 2, one can see that that job security has increased for virtually all demographic groups, and that these changes have not been uniform.

EU transition rates

Although there was a strong decline in the overall EU transition rate, the decline was not uniform. The decline in the EU transition rate was larger (both in relative and absolute terms) for men than for women. Among men, the decline in the EU transition rate was concentrated among younger workers (19-24 and 25-34 year-olds). There was no statistically significant change for 35-44 year-olds, and the EU transition rate for 45-54 year-olds actually increased. Initial EU transition rates were monotonically decreasing in age, so that these trends have tended to equalize EU transition rates across age groups. For women the changes were more evenly distributed. The EU transition rate fell for every age group except 35-44 year-olds, who did not see any statistically significant change.

---

unemployment are not affected.

All education levels saw a decrease in EU transition rates during this time period. For men, the decrease in EU transition rates was larger among High School Graduates and those with Some College. Employment-to-unemployment transition rates also decreased among High School Dropouts and College Graduates, but the decreases were not as dramatic. Among women, the decline in the EU transition rate monotonically increased with education, with High School Dropouts seeing no change. These trends tended to magnify initial differences across education levels.

The EU transition rate fell significantly for married men and women. The percentage point decrease in the EU transition rate was over twice as large for unmarried men, but relative decline was about the same for the two groups. Among women the decline, both the percentage point decline and the relative decline, was larger for married women than for unmarried women.

The relative decline in the EU transition rate was larger for whites than for nonwhites. Initially, the EU transition rate for nonwhite men was about 31 percent higher than the rate for whites. The absolute difference has remained about the same, which means that the relative gap has increased.

These trends indicate that job security has increased for nearly all demographic groups, and that there were significant differences across groups. In some cases, these differences tended to equalize differences across groups, while in other cases the differences magnified differences.

EE transition rates

The most dramatic trend has been the sharp increase in EE transition rates. The EE transition rate increased by 45 percent for men and by 58 percent for women. As one would expect, initial EE transition rates monotonically decreased with age, reflecting the fact that workers job shop early in their careers and gradually settle into more permanent jobs. However, trends in EE transition rates have worked in the opposite direction. For both men and women, the relative increase in the EE transition rate increased with age, with the rates for 45-54 year-old men and women more than doubling. Younger workers still change jobs more frequently, but these trends have narrowed the gap considerably.

By education, the changes were more uniformly distributed, and there were some differences between men and women. As expected, initial EE transition rates were lower for less educated workers.[26] Among women, the large relative increase in the EE transition rate among less educated women tended to narrow the initial differences across education levels, while for men the pattern was less clear. The trends narrowed the differences between the rates for High School Graduates and men with Some College relative to the rate for College Graduates. Although the EE transition rate for male High School Dropouts increased over the period, the increase was smaller than for more educated workers.

By race, the EE transition rate increased more, both relatively and absolutely, for nonwhites than for whites. Given the higher initial EE transition rates among whites, these trends have tended to equalize rates.

Married men and women saw the greatest relative increase in EE transition rates, with the difference between the two groups being greater for men than for women. These changes virtually eliminated differences between married and unmarried men, and narrowed the relative gap between married and unmarried women.

The increase in EE transition rates suggests that it has become easier to change jobs, and that on-the-job search may have become a more important phenomenon.

---

[26] This finding is consistent with Royalty (1998). It is also consistent with the findings of Hyson and Polivka (2001), who find that on-the-job search is more prevalent among more educated workers.

EN transition rates

The changes in EN transition rates were fairly predictable--there was a slight increase (not statistically significant) among men and a large decline among women. For men, the EN transition rate increased among less educated workers (High School Dropouts and High School Graduates), and declined or remained constant among more educated workers (men with Some College and College Graduates). Nonwhite and married men also experienced increases. The absence of any statistically significant increase in the overall EN transition rate is consistent with Juhn's (1992) finding that most of the increase in the nonemployment rate of men can be explained by a decline in nonemployment-to-employment transitions rather than an increase in employment-to-nonemployment transitions. Among women, the EN transition rate declined for all groups except 19-24 year-olds and single women. Perhaps the most notable pattern is that the relative decline in the EN transition rate increased with education. There was a similar pattern by age. The two oldest age groups, who initially had the lowest EN transition rates, saw the greatest relative decline. Hence, trends in EN transition rates magnified the initial differences between older and younger women and between more educated and less educated women.

Did Job Stability and Job Security Decline in the 1990s?

The short answer is no. Overall job stability increased slightly, while job security increased significantly. Table 3 shows the coefficient from probit equations estimated over the 1988-2000 period. The equations are identical to the ones in Table 1 except for the time period. Table 4 shows the change over the 1988-2000 period as a percentage of transition rates in 1988. Comparing the coefficients and percentages in Tables 3 and 4 to those in Tables 1 and 2, one can see that the 1988-2000 period looks considerably different from the 1975-2000 period, indicating significant changes in the 1990s.

The EU transition rate of both men and women continued to decline in the 1990s. For men, the coefficient in Table 3 is more than twice the coefficient in Table 1 implying that nearly all of the decline in the EU transition rate occurred in the 1990s. In contrast, the rate of decline for women was about the same for the 1988-2000 period as it was for the entire 1975-2000 period, indicating that about half of the decline occurred in the 1990s.

Looking at the trends by age, education, race and marital status reveals more differences. In the 1990s, trends in the EU transition rates of men have tended to magnify differences by age, education, race, and marital status. This is in contrast to 1975-2000 period, during which the trends tended to narrow differences by age and maintain differences by race and marital status. Among women, the trends were more similar to those of the 1975-2000 period. The trends by education group generally narrowed differences in the 1990s, in contrast to magnification of differences that occurred over the entire 1975-2000 period. By race and marital status, the trends continued to magnify differences across groups.

In contrast to the EU transition rate, the increase in the EE transition rate slowed down considerably in the 1990s. One can see that the slowdown was fairly uniform across groups, with a number of groups showing no statistically significant change during the 1990s. This is in sharp contrast to the dramatic increases for the entire 1975-2000 period, and indicates that most of the increase in EE transition rates occurred in the late 1970s and the 1980s.

A look at EN transition rates reveals a few surprises. The EN transition rate for women remained essentially constant during the 1990s, and there was virtually no variation across groups. Married women were the only group to deviate, having experienced a slight decrease in their EN transition rate. Among men, the overall EN transition rate increased significantly, but this increase is entirely due to a downward blip in the EN transition rate in 1988. When the equations are reestimated over the 1989-2001 period the overall EN transition rate for men does not exhibit any statistically significant upward trend, although the EN transition rates for 35-44 year-olds and High School Graduates continued to increase. The coefficients for these two groups were significantly larger in the 1989-2001 regressions indicating an acceleration of the rate of increase for these groups.

Married Couples

Looking at married couples as single entities required just a few straightforward modifications to the sample inclusion criteria and the transition definitions. A couple is included in the sample if either spouse was included in the sample of individuals. Defining transitions was a little more complicated, because I focus on jobs that are important to the economic security of the couple. A couple is considered to have experienced a transition if at least one spouse met the following conditions: the spouse was included in the sample of individuals, the spouse earned at least 40 percent of the couple's total earnings, and the spouse experienced the transition in question. It is important to recognize that, in contrast to the transitions of individuals, the component transitions are not mutually exclusive. For example, the wife could have experienced an EE transition, while the husband experienced an EN transition. As above, separate equations were run for each transition, so this couple would show up as having experienced both an EE and an EN transition in the respective equations.

Table 5 shows the coefficients from probit equations estimated over the sample of married couples. All equations include a time trend variable as well as dummy variables to control for race (white/nonwhite), husband's and wife's age (4 categories each), husband's and wife's education (4 categories each), and region (4 categories). To simplify presentation, I have omitted the coefficients on the control variables. The top row of Table 5 contains coefficients on

-19-

the time trend variable for each transition. The second row is the same as the first, except that it includes controls for the composition of earner categories. Subsequent rows contain coefficients on the time trend variable interacted with three earner category variables (husband primary earner, wife primary earner, equal earner). All coefficients are expressed as marginal effects. The bottom panel of Table 5 shows the change over the 1975-2000 period as a percentage of the 1975 transition rates.

Between 1975 and 2000, the trends in transition rates for couples were very similar to those for individuals. There was a moderate increase in the separation rate, which was the result of a large increase in the EE transition rate, a moderate decrease in the EU transition rate, and a slight decrease in the EN transition rate.

The decline in EU transition rates indicates that job security increased for all earner categories. Wife primary-earner couples saw the largest decline, which tended to narrow the difference in transition rates between wife primary-earner and husband primary-earner couples. There was a moderate decline in the EU transition rate of equal-earner couples, but, not surprisingly, their EU transition rate is still considerably higher than the rates for wife primary-earner and husband primary-earner couples. If the distribution of earner categories had remained the same, the EU transition rate would have declined by 21 percent rather than 16. Hence, it appears that the shift toward two-earner couples has worked in the direction of reducing job security, rather than increasing it.

As was the case for individuals, there was a dramatic increase in EE transition rates. All earner categories saw substantial increases, with the rate for wife primary-earner couples doubling. These trends have equalized the EE transition rates of wife primary-earner and husband primary-earner couples. Not surprisingly, the EE transition rate for equal-earner couples is still higher than for the other types, but the difference is much smaller. It is worth noting that some of the overall increase in the EE transition rate is due to changes in the distribution of types. Controlling for composition, the increase in the overall EE transition rate was 52 percent versus the actual change of 61 percent.

The slight increase in the overall EN transition rate primarily was due to the increase in the fraction of wife primary-earner and equal-earner couples, who have higher EN transition rates. The EN transition rate of husband primary-earner couples doubled, but their initial EN transition rates were so low (an order of magnitude smaller than the other earner categories) that the increase had little effect on the overall rate. If there had been no change in composition, the EN transition rate would have fallen by 11 instead of increasing by 6 percent. Hence, the decline in EN transitions among wife primary-earner and equal-earner couples was not enough to offset the effect of compositional changes.

Looking at the coefficients in the right panel of Table 5, one can see that there were some changes in the 1990s. The EE transition rate increased at a slightly faster rate (in absolute terms) in the 1990s, and was due to an acceleration in the rate for husband primary-earner couples. Other earner categories saw a sharp deceleration in their EE transition rates. The decline in the EU transition rate accelerated. Again, this acceleration was due to husband primary-earner couples. There appears to have been a slight acceleration in the increase in the EN transition rate among husband primary-earner couples, but, as noted above, this acceleration is due to the downward blip in the EN transition rate in 1988. When I reestimated the probit equation over the 1989-2001 period, there was no statistically significant change in the EN transition rate of husband primary-earner couples. Nor was there a statistically significant change in the EN transition rate for wife primary-earner couples and equal-earner couples, which implies that the decline in the EN transition rate among married women was due to a decline among women whose earnings comprise less than 40 percent of the couples earnings.

V. Discussion and Conclusions

The evidence presented here indicates that job stability, as measured by separation rates, has remained constant over the 1975-2000 period, but that there have been significant changes in the component transitions. Employment-to-unemployment transition rates have fallen, and EE transition rates have increased. The decreases in EU transition rates were not uniform across groups. Among men, the trends tended to narrow initial differences by age, while the trends for women tended to magnify initial differences by education. Interestingly, much of the decline in EU transition rates occurred in the 1990s. About half the decline for women and nearly all of the decline among men occurred in the 1990s.

As with EU transitions, the increases in EE transition rates were not uniform across groups, and these differences tended to narrow differences across groups. Among men, trends in EE transition rates tended to equalize differences by age, and for women trends in EE transition rates tended to narrow differences by education level. In the 1990s, the increase in EE transition rates slowed considerably. It is interesting to note that, over this period, the job-change rate (the fraction of workers who had two or more employers during the previous year) remained fairly constant. But there was a significant increase in the fraction job changers who experienced two or fewer weeks of unemployment, and a similar decrease in the fraction that experienced three or more weeks of unemployment. Hence, a much larger fraction of job changes are now occurring without any intervening spell of unemployment. This suggests that on-the-job search may have become more important since 1975, and that there may have been a decrease in the natural rate of unemployment.

The trends in EN transition rates were fairly predictable. Over the 1975-2000 period there were large declines for women, while the rates for men did not change. However, the 1990s appear to be different. The EN transition rate for women remained essentially constant, indicating that virtually all of the decline in EN transition rates occurred before 1988. And the EN transition rate for men began to increase. There were large increases in the EN transition rates of 35-44 year-old men and male high school graduates.

Looking at married couples I found that job stability decreased, but that job security increased. The overall separation rate increased moderately, which was due to a large increase in the EE transition rate, a moderate decrease in the EU transition rate, and a slight decrease in the EN transition rate. Although most of these changes in transition rates were due to within-group changes, changes in the composition of earner categories (husband primary-earner, wife primary-earner, and equal-earner) away from husband primary-earner couples played a role. This compositional change resulted in a larger increase in the separation rate and the EE transition rate, and in the smaller decrease in the EU transition rate. Thus, it appears that the shift away from husband primary-earner couples has worked in the direction of reducing job stability and security for married couples.

Appendix

Using Industry Codes to Detect Job Changes

It is possible to use changes in the industry code to determine whether a job change occurred because industry and occupation are dependently coded. The interviewer determines whether the respondent's longest job last year is the same as the main job last week based on the verbatim descriptions of the two jobs, and probes when necessary. If the jobs are the same, the interviewer marks a check item and the longest job last year was given the same 3-digit industry and occupation codes as the main job last week.[27] If not, the industry and occupation codes are collected as usual (that is, independently). The advantage of dependent coding is that it greatly reduces the number of spurious changes in industry and occupation codes.

Unfortunately, the CPS defines a job as a position, so that industry and occupation are supposed to be coded independently if a worker gets a promotion or has some other within employer job change. This implies that changes in occupation that are not accompanied by a change in industry may be within-employer job changes. It is for this reason that I use only the industry code to identify a job change.

Next, I had to determine whether to use 1-, 2-, or 3-digit industry codes. The level of coding is important, because with independent industry coding it is possible to generate spurious job changes. Tests connected with the CPS redesign show that independent coding at the 3-digit level results in a large number of spurious transitions. Month-to-month changes in 3-digit industry codes were 23 percent, compared with the estimated true changes of 3.8-4.2 percent.[28] Given the high number of spurious transitions that would result, I do not use changes in 3-digit

---

[27] Unfortunately, the check item is not on the March tapes.

industry codes to detect changes in employment. Using 2-digit codes resulted in nearly as many job changes, but the number fell off considerably for 1-digit industry codes. Hence, I took the conservative approach of using 1-digit industry codes to determine whether a worker changed employers.[29]

Unfortunately, the CPS defines a job as a position, so that industry and occupation are coded independently if a worker gets a promotion or has some other within-employer job change. Hence, changes in occupation that are not accompanied by a change in industry are most likely within-employer job changes, which is why I use only the industry code to identify a job change. But with independent coding it is possible for the industry code to change even if the worker did not change employers. Hence, the question becomes whether to use 1-, 2-, or 3-digit industry codes. Tests connected with the 1994 redesign of the CPS show that independent coding at the 3-digit level results in a large number of spurious transitions. Month-to-month changes in 3-digit industry codes were 23 percent, compared with estimated true changes of 3.8-4.2 percent.[30] Given the high number of spurious transitions that would result, I do not use changes in 3-digit industry codes to detect changes in employment. Using 2-digit codes resulted in nearly as many job changes, but the number fell off considerably for 1-digit industry codes. Given this, I took the conservative approach of using 1-digit industry codes to determine whether a worker changed employers.

---

[28] When industry was dependently coded, the month-to-month changes fell to 5 percent (see Polivka and Rothgeb 1993).

[29] I experimented with several ways of defining turnover. Although there were differences in levels (as expected) the trends were remarkably similar. Table 6 shows the results of linear time trend regressions on alternative measures of turnover.

[30] When industry was dependently coded, the month-to-month changes fell to 5 percent (see Polivka and Rothgeb [1993]).

Changes in Census Imputation Procedures

In 1989, the Census Bureau changed the procedures it uses to impute missing data. Prior to 1989, the Census Bureau imputed industry and occupation codes in one of two ways. First, if only a few income and labor market history variables were missing, then each variable was imputed separately. Industry and occupation codes were carried over from the current job from the Basic CPS. This imputation procedure misses actual changes in industry and occupation codes, which results in an underestimate of the number of job changes. The second method of imputing industry and occupation codes tends to generate spurious job changes. The Census Bureau separated the income and work history variables into two groups; variables about earned income, and variables about unearned income. If more than a few variables were missing from either group, Census would impute all variables of that group from a single observation. This was done to make the variables in the group internally consistent. However, when the earned income variables were imputed as a group, industry and occupation codes were very likely to change, which would cause me to overestimate job changes. Unfortunately, there are no allocation flags for industry and occupation prior to 1989, so it is impossible to correct for these imputation procedures. However, it is likely that the effect of these procedures is fairly constant over time. Although these procedures may affect my estimates of the level of the job change rate, they should not affect comparisons across demographic groups or changes over time.

In 1989, the Census bureau changed it allocation procedures and began allocating entire records. The advantage of this type of allocation is that all of the income data are internally consistent within an observation. A disadvantage is that often good data are thrown away. The Census Bureau imputes industry and occupation codes along with other work and income data, even if industry and occupation codes are available or could have been imputed from the current year's data.

The introduction of these FL-665 observations would not be a particular problem for my purposes if these were used instead of the imputation-by-groups-of-variables approach described above. If this were the case, there would be no significant changes in spurious job changes. However, Census changed the criteria by which data were allocated. Under the new system a larger fraction of industry and occupation codes were allocated using the hot deck procedure than in previous years. Between about 9.5 and about 13.5 percent of all records are Type A allocations. With no correction, this change would have had the effect of significantly increasing the separation and job change rates.

References

Abraham, Katharine G. (1997) "Comment on Farber 'The Changing Face of Job Loss in the United States: 1981-1995,'" *Brookings Papers on Economic Activity: Microeconomics*, in press.

Bansak, Cynthia and Steven Raphael (1998) "Have Employment Relationships in the United States Become Less Stable?" Discussion Paper 98-15, UC San Diego.

Boisjoly, Johanne, Greg J. Duncan, and Timothy Smeeding (1998) "The Shifting Incidence of Involuntary Job Losses from 1968 to 1992," *Industrial Relations* 37(2), April 1998, pp. 207-31.

Diebold, Francis X., David Neumark, and Daniel Polsky (1997) "Job Stability in the United States," *Journal of Labor Economics* 15(2), April 1997, pp. 206-33.

Diebold, Francis X., David Neumark, and Daniel Polsky (1996) "Comment on Kenneth A. Swinnerton and Howard Wial, 'Is Job Stability Declining in the U.S. Economy?'" *Industrial and Labor Relations Review* 49(2), January 1996, pp. 348-352.

Evans, David S. and Linda S. Leighton (1995) "Retrospective Bias in the Displaced Worker Surveys," *Journal of Human Resources* 30(2), Spring 1995, pp.386-196.

Farber, Henry S. (1997a) "The Changing Face of Job Loss in the United States: 1981-1995," *Brookings Papers on Economic Activity: Microeconomics*, in press.

Farber, Henry S. (1997b) "Trends in Long Term Employment in the United States, 1979-96," unpublished manuscript, Princeton University, June 1997.

Farber, Henry S. (1997c) "Has the Rate of Job Loss Increased Over Time?" unpublished manuscript, Princeton University, December 1997.

Farber, Henry S. (1998) "Are Lifetime Jobs Disappearing? Job Duration in the United States: 1973-1993," in *Labor Statistics Measurement Issues*, John Haltiwanger, Marilyn Manser, and Robert Topel, eds., University of Chicago Press.

Farber, Henry S. (2001) "Job Loss in the United States, 1981-1999" unpublished manuscript, Princeton University, January 2001.

Fitzgerald, John (1999) "Job Instability and Earnings and Income Consequences: Evidence from SIPP 1983-1995," unpublished manuscript, Bowdoin College, July 1999.

Gottschalk, P. and R. Moffitt (1994) "The Growth of Earnings Instability in the U.S. Labor Market," *Brookings Papers on Economic Activity* 2:1994, pp.217-272.

Gottschalk, P. and R. Moffitt (1994) "Changes in Job Instability and Insecurity Using Monthly Survey Data," *Journal of Labor Economics* 17(2, pt. 2), October 1999, pp. S91-127.

Jaeger, David (1997) "Reconciling the Old and New Census Bureau Education Questions: Recommendations for Researchers," *Journal of Business and Economic Statistics* 15(3), pp. 300-9.

Jaeger, David and Ann Huff Stevens (1997) "Is Job Stability in the United States Falling? Trends in the Current Population Survey and Panel Study of Income Dynamics," *Journal of Labor Economics* 17(2, pt. 2), October 1999, pp. S1-28.

Juhn, Chinhui. (1992) " The Decline Of Male Labor Market Participation: The Role of Declining Market Opportunities," *Quarterly Journal of Economics* 107(1), February 1992, pp. 79-121.

Katz, Lawrence and Kevin M. Murphy (1992) "Changes in the Wage Structure 1963-1987: Supply and Demand Factors," *Quarterly Journal of Economics* 107(1), February 1992, pp. 35-78.

Marcotte, D. (1996) "Has Job Stability Declined?: Evidence from the Panel Study of Income Dynamics," unpublished manuscript, Northern Illinois University, February 1996.

Monks, James, and Steven Pizer (1997) "Trends in Voluntary and Involuntary Job Turnover," *Industrial Relations* 37(4), October 1998, pp. 440-59.

Murphy, Kevin M. and Finis Welch (1992) "The Structure of Wages," *Quarterly Journal of Economics* 107(1), February 1992, pp. 285-326.

Neumark, David and Daniel Polsky (1998) "Changes in Job Stability and Job Security: Anecdotes and Evidence" in the Proceedings of the 50th Annual IRRA Meetings.

Neumark, David, Daniel Polsky, and Daniel Hansen (1998) "Has Job Stability Declined Yet? New Evidence for the 1990s," *Journal of Labor Economics* 17(2, pt. 2), October 1999, pp. S29-64.

Polivka, Anne E. and Rosemary Hyson (2001) "Predictors and Payoffs of On-the-Job Search," unpublished manuscript, Bureau of Labor Statistics, November 2001.

Polivka, Anne E. and Steven Miller (1998) "The CPS After the Redesign: Refocusing the Economic Lens," in *Labor Statistics Measurement Issues*, John Haltiwanger, Marilyn Manser, and Robert Topel, eds., University of Chicago Press.

Polivka, Anne E. and Jennifer Rothgeb (1993) "Redesigning the Questionnaire," *Monthly Labor Review* 116(9), September 1993, pp. 10-28.

Polsky, Daniel (1999) "Changes in the Consequences of Job Separations in the U.S. Economy," *Industrial and Labor Relations Review* 52(4), July 1999, pp. 565-580.

Rose, Stephen (1995) "Declining Job Security and the Professionalization of Opportunity," National Commission for Employment Policy, Research Report 95-4, April 1995.

Royalty, Ann Beeson (1998) "Job-to-Job and Job-toNonemployment Turnover by Gender and Education Level," Journal of Labor Economics 16(2), April 1998, pp. 392-443.

Ruhm, Christopher (1991) "Are Workers Permanently Scarred by Job Displacements?" *American Economic Review* 81(1), March 1991, pp. 319-24.

Stewart, Jay (1998) "Has Job Mobility Increased? Evidence from the Current Population Survey: 1975-1995," BLS Working Paper #308.

Stewart, Jay (2000) "Did Job Security Decline in the 1990s?" in *On the Job: Is Long-Term Employment a Thing of the Past?* D. Neumark, ed., Russell Sage Foundation.

Swinnerton, Kenneth A. and Howard Wial (1995) "Is Job Stability Declining in the U.S. Economy?" *Industrial and Labor Relations Review* 48(2) January 1995, pp. 293-304.

Swinnerton, Kenneth A. and Howard Wial (1996) "Is Job Stability Declining in the U.S. Economy? Reply to Diebold, Neumark, and Polsky" *Industrial and Labor Relations Review* 48(2) January 1996, pp. 352-355.

Valletta, Robert (1998) "Declining Job Security," *Journal of Labor Economics* 17(2, pt. 2), October 1999, pp. S170-97.

Yakoboski, Paul (1997) "Large Plan Lump-Sums: Rollovers and Cashouts," Employee Benefit Research Institute *Issue Brief* Number 188, August 1997.

Figure1. All workers

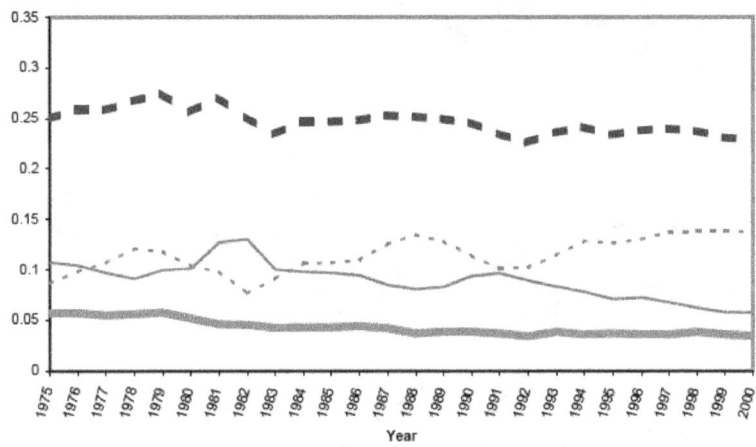

Figure 2. Men

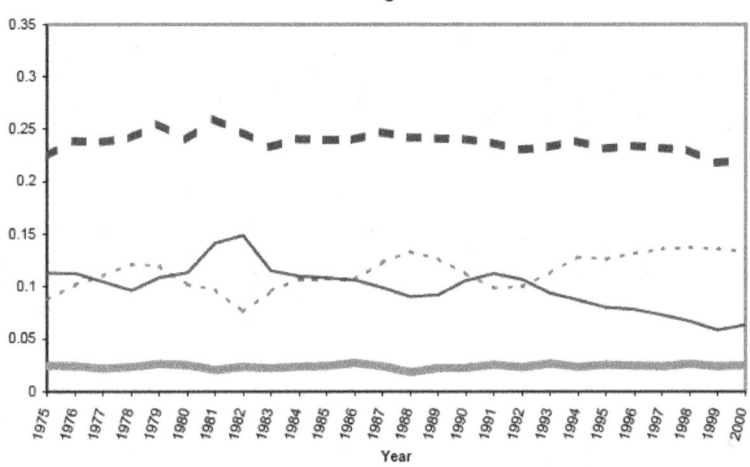

Figure 3. Women

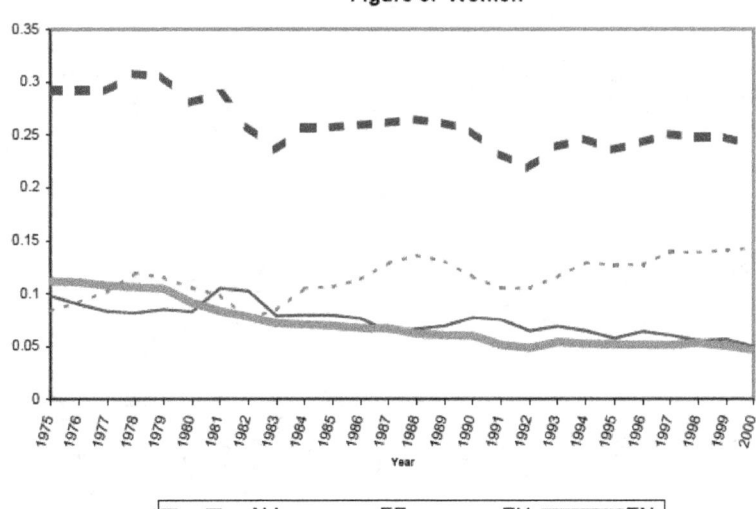

ALL · · · · · · EE ——— EU ▬▬▬ EN

Table 1. Trends in Job Separation Rates - 1975-2000

Marginal Effects Estimated from Probit Equations

	Men				Women			
	All Separations	EE	EU	EN	All Separations	EE	EU	EN
All	0.0004 **	0.0016 **	-0.0013 **	0.0001	-0.0003 *	0.0020 **	-0.0008 **	-0.0014 **
	(0.0001)	(0.0001)	(0.0001)	(0.0000)	(0.0001)	(0.0001)	(0.0001)	(0.0001)
Age								
19-24	-0.0013 **	0.0014 **	-0.0026 **	0.0003 **	-0.0001	0.0016 **	-0.0012 **	-0.0002
	(0.0003)	(0.0002)	(0.0001)	(0.0000)	(0.0003)	(0.0002)	(0.0001)	(0.0001)
25-34	-0.0011 **	0.0011 **	-0.0021 **	-0.0002 **	-0.0013 **	0.0021 **	-0.0011 **	-0.0020 **
	(0.0002)	(0.0001)	(0.0001)	(0.0001)	(0.0003)	(0.0001)	(0.0001)	(0.0001)
35-44	0.0020 **	0.0020 **	-0.0002	0.0002 **	-0.0001	0.0015 **	-0.0003	-0.0014 **
	(0.0002)	(0.0001)	(0.0001)	(0.0001)	(0.0002)	(0.0001)	(0.0001)	(0.0001)
45-54	0.0025 **	0.0022 **	0.0003 *	0.0000	0.0010 **	0.0027 **	-0.0004 **	-0.0012 **
	(0.0002)	(0.0001)	(0.0001)	(0.0001)	(0.0002)	(0.0002)	(0.0001)	(0.0001)
Education								
High School Dropouts	-0.0006 *	0.0008 **	-0.0011 **	0.0003 **	-0.0009 **	0.0017 **	-0.0003	-0.0010 **
	(0.0002)	(0.0002)	(0.0001)	(0.0001)	(0.0003)	(0.0003)	(0.0002)	(0.0002)
High School	0.0003	0.0017 **	-0.0014 **	0.0002 **	-0.0005 **	0.0021 **	-0.0009 **	-0.0013 **
	(0.0002)	(0.0001)	(0.0001)	(0.0001)	(0.0003)	(0.0001)	(0.0002)	(0.0002)
Some College	0.0001	0.0019 **	-0.0018 **	-0.0002 **	-0.0003	0.0021 **	-0.0010 **	-0.0015 **
	(0.0002)	(0.0001)	(0.0001)	(0.0001)	(0.0002)	(0.0001)	(0.0001)	(0.0001)
College Graduates	0.0017	0.0016 **	-0.0004 **	-0.0001	0.0004	0.0018 **	-0.0007 **	-0.0018 **
	(0.0002)	(0.0001)	(0.0001)	(0.0001)	(0.0002)	(0.0002)	(0.0001)	(0.0002)
Race								
White	0.0004 **	0.0016 **	-0.0013 **	0.0000	-0.0007 **	0.0017 **	-0.0009 **	-0.0015 **
	(0.0001)	(0.0001)	(0.0001)	(0.0001)	(0.0001)	(0.0001)	(0.0001)	(0.0001)
Nonwhite	0.0004	0.0017 **	-0.0013 **	0.0003 **	0.0014 **	0.0033 **	-0.0005 **	-0.0007 **
	(0.0003)	(0.0002)	(0.0002)	(0.0001)	(0.0002)	(0.0002)	(0.0001)	(0.0002)
Marital Status								
Married-spouse present	0.0012 **	0.0017 **	-0.0009 **	0.0001 *	-0.0019 **	0.0017 **	-0.0009 **	-0.0021 **
	(0.0001)	(0.0001)	(0.0001)	(0.0000)	(0.0002)	(0.0001)	(0.0001)	(0.0001)
Other	-0.0008 **	0.0015 **	-0.0018 **	0.0000	0.0017 **	0.0022 **	-0.0007 **	0.0000
	(0.0002)	(0.0001)	(0.0001)	(0.0000)	(0.0002)	(0.0001)	(0.0001)	(0.0001)

Note: Standard errors are in parentheses. ** indicates significance at the 1-percent level. * indicates significance at the 5-percent level. Separate equations were run for each group of variables, and each equation includes dummy variables to control for race, age, education, marital status, and region.

Table 2. Change over 1975-2000 period (as a percentage of 1975 transition rates)

	Men				Women			
	All Separations	EE	EU	EN	All Separations	EE	EU	EN
All	4.56%	45.22%	-28.50%	5.35%	-2.71%	58.47%	-20.30%	-30.49%
Age								
19-24	-7.54%	25.44%	-25.73%	12.49%	-0.67%	30.33%	-16.89%	-2.86%
25-34	-10.27%	23.23%	-43.78%	-17.40%	-9.44%	54.53%	-29.70%	-34.78%
35-44	33.81%	78.67%	-8.55%	37.09%	-0.72%	52.18%	-8.85%	-53.71%
45-54	51.43%	144.08%	13.57%	-1.46%	15.22%	190.11%	-19.10%	-46.88%
Education								
High School Dropouts	-5.08%	23.40%	-18.40%	18.89%	-6.25%	69.39%	-5.28%	-14.47%
High School	3.37%	59.50%	-28.00%	32.90%	-4.75%	67.71%	-21.72%	-32.98%
Some College	1.02%	47.21%	-40.55%	-12.95%	-2.38%	47.59%	-26.27%	-33.03%
College Graduates	24.57%	35.52%	-21.42%	-24.84%	4.39%	41.83%	-34.57%	-65.95%
Race								
White	4.68%	43.62%	-29.48%	0.39%	-5.67%	48.41%	-22.28%	-33.51%
Nonwhite	3.75%	61.71%	-22.38%	19.77%	13.05%	146.64%	-12.53%	-15.88%
Marital Status								
Married-spouse present	15.92%	50.56%	-25.50%	20.28%	-16.41%	61.01%	-26.98%	-38.72%
Other	-5.80%	34.82%	-23.52%	0.07%	13.93%	52.52%	-14.12%	-0.65%

Table 3. Trends in Job Separation Rates - 1988-2000

Marginal Effects Estimated from Probit Equations

	Men				Women			
	All Separations	EE	EU	EN	All Separations	EE	EU	EN
All	-0.0007 * (0.0003)	0.0012 ** (0.0002)	-0.0024 ** (0.0002)	0.0004 ** (0.0001)	-0.0001 (0.0004)	0.0012 ** (0.0002)	-0.0009 ** (0.0002)	-0.0003 (0.0002)
Age								
19-24	-0.0009 (0.0008)	-0.0004 (0.0006)	-0.0018 ** (0.0002)	0.0009 ** (0.0002)	0.0001 (0.0009)	0.0000 (0.0007)	-0.0002 (0.0005)	0.0003 (0.0004)
25-34	-0.0017 ** (0.0005)	0.0007 * (0.0004)	-0.0027 ** (0.0002)	0.0001 (0.0002)	0.0000 (0.0009)	0.0015 ** (0.0007)	-0.0012 ** (0.0005)	-0.0003 (0.0004)
35-44	0.0000 (0.0005)	0.0023 ** (0.0004)	-0.0030 ** (0.0003)	0.0006 ** (0.0002)	-0.0009 (0.0006)	0.0008 (0.0004)	-0.0011 ** (0.0003)	-0.0005 (0.0003)
45-54	0.0003 (0.0007)	0.0014 ** (0.0005)	-0.0012 ** (0.0004)	0.0000 (0.0002)	0.0009 (0.0006)	0.0021 ** (0.0005)	-0.0005 (0.0003)	-0.0006 (0.0003)
Education								
High School Dropouts	-0.0048 ** (0.0008)	0.0001 (0.0007)	-0.0032 ** (0.0004)	0.0001 (0.0002)	-0.0001 (0.0011)	0.0018 ** (0.0006)	0.0004 (0.0005)	-0.0008 (0.0004)
High School	-0.0015 ** (0.0005)	0.0008 * (0.0004)	-0.0024 ** (0.0003)	0.0007 ** (0.0002)	0.0000 (0.0006)	0.0013 ** (0.0005)	-0.0011 ** (0.0003)	0.0002 (0.0003)
Some College	0.0000 (0.0005)	0.0017 ** (0.0004)	-0.0024 ** (0.0003)	0.0003 (0.0002)	-0.0006 (0.0006)	0.0013 ** (0.0005)	-0.0014 ** (0.0003)	-0.0005 (0.0003)
College Graduates	0.0018 ** (0.0006)	0.0017 ** (0.0004)	-0.0014 ** (0.0004)	0.0003 (0.0002)	0.0004 (0.0007)	0.0008 (0.0005)	-0.0006 (0.0004)	-0.0005 (0.0004)
Race								
White	-0.0005 (0.0003)	0.0011 ** (0.0003)	-0.0023 ** (0.0002)	0.0004 ** (0.0001)	-0.0003 (0.0004)	0.0010 ** (0.0003)	-0.0010 ** (0.0002)	-0.0004 (0.0002)
Nonwhite	-0.0020 ** (0.0008)	0.0015 * (0.0006)	-0.0028 ** (0.0005)	0.0003 (0.0002)	0.0012 (0.0008)	0.0023 ** (0.0006)	-0.0005 (0.0004)	0.0000 (0.0002)
Other	-0.0023 ** (0.0005)	0.0004 (0.0004)	-0.0025 ** (0.0003)	0.0004 ** (0.0001)	0.0013 ** (0.0005)	0.0016 ** (0.0004)	-0.0007 ** (0.0003)	0.0004 (0.0003)
Marital Status								
Married-spouse present	0.0005 (0.0004)	0.0017 ** (0.0003)	-0.0022 ** (0.0003)	0.0003 * (0.0001)	-0.0013 ** (0.0005)	0.0008 * (0.0004)	-0.0011 ** (0.0003)	-0.0008 ** (0.0002)

Note: Standard errors are in parentheses. ** indicates significance at the 1-percent level. * indicates significance at the 5-percent level. Separate equations were run for each group of variables, and each equation includes dummy variables to control for race, age, education, marital status, and region.

Table 4. Change over 1988-2000 period (as a percentage of 1988 transition rates)

	Men				Women			
	All Separations	EE	EU	EN	All Separations	EE	EU	EN
All	-3.54%	10.66%	-31.31%	25.65%	-0.24%	10.47%	-16.29%	-5.89%
Age								
19-24	-2.59%	-2.01%	-12.64%	25.47%	-0.24%	-0.24%	-1.99%	2.93%
25-34	-7.24%	5.28%	-31.03%	11.28%	0.16%	11.25%	-21.14%	-5.43%
35-44	-0.21%	28.77%	-49.47%	72.20%	-5.18%	9.24%	-25.12%	-15.21%
45-54	2.09%	23.38%	-29.28%	1.34%	6.52%	26.71%	-15.88%	-17.45%
Education								
High School Dropouts	-16.99%	0.74%	-22.15%	4.13%	-0.23%	20.24%	4.76%	-6.77%
High School	-7.04%	7.25%	-26.72%	62.97%	0.20%	12.68%	-18.07%	4.00%
Some College	0.23%	13.90%	-37.99%	13.90%	-2.48%	10.54%	-28.56%	-9.73%
College Graduates	12.68%	15.53%	-43.81%	41.25%	2.00%	5.88%	-15.55%	-15.86%
Race								
White	-2.48%	9.97%	-32.09%	29.68%	-1.54%	8.11%	-19.38%	-7.08%
Nonwhite	-9.11%	16.47%	-26.37%	11.84%	5.91%	26.35%	-7.12%	-0.62%
Marital Status								
Married-spouse present	2.92%	18.32%	-42.19%	37.76%	-6.19%	8.09%	-26.48%	-13.17%
Other	-8.09%	2.60%	-21.38%	16.00%	5.53%	12.04%	-9.52%	12.25%

Table 5. Couples Equations

Trends in Job Separation Rates
(Marginal Effects Estimated from Probit Equations)

	1975 - 2000				1988 - 2000			
	All Separations	EE	EU	EN	All Separations	EE	EU	EN
All	0.0016 **	0.0021 **	-0.0006 **	0.0001 *	0.0015 **	0.0022 **	-0.0012 **	0.0003
	(0.0001)	(0.0001)	(0.0000)	(0.0000)	(0.0004)	(0.0003)	(0.0002)	(0.0001)
All (controling for composition)	0.0008 **	0.0017 **	-0.0008 **	-0.0002 **	0.0011 **	0.0020 **	-0.0013 **	0.0001
	(0.0001)	(0.0001)	(0.0001)	(0.0000)	(0.0004)	(0.0003)	(0.0002)	(0.0001)
Earner class								
Male primary	0.0014 **	0.0015 **	-0.0006 **	0.0005 **	0.0017 **	0.0024 **	-0.0014 **	0.0006 **
	(0.0001)	(0.0001)	(0.0001)	(0.0001)	(0.0004)	(0.0003)	(0.0002)	(0.0001)
Female primary	-0.0008 *	0.0023 **	-0.0009 **	-0.0006 **	0.0001	0.0009	-0.0003	-0.0001
	(0.0003)	(0.0003)	(0.0002)	(0.0001)	(0.0010)	(0.0008)	(0.0006)	(0.0003)
Equal earner	0.0000	0.0020 **	-0.0011 **	-0.0007 **	0.0003	0.0015 **	-0.0014 **	-0.0002
	(0.0002)	(0.0003)	(0.0001)	(0.0001)	(0.0006)	(0.0004)	(0.0003)	(0.0002)

Change Over Period
(as a percentage of initial year transition rates)

	1975 - 2000				1988 - 2000			
	All Separations	EE	EU	EN	All Separations	EE	EU	EN
All	19.22%	61.25%	-16.22%	5.94%	18.67%	46.16%	-49.82%	22.61%
All (controling for composition)	10.05%	51.69%	-21.00%	-11.49%	13.32%	41.37%	-52.93%	9.86%
Earner class								
Male primary	21.64%	51.63%	-18.95%	106.55%	27.60%	65.58%	-68.31%	173.93%
Female primary	-7.57%	103.36%	-25.01%	-12.35%	1.27%	19.94%	-21.85%	-1.83%
Equal earner	0.01%	37.47%	-18.16%	-13.96%	2.21%	18.88%	-34.61%	-7.32%

www.ingramcontent.com/pod-product-compliance
Lightning Source LLC
Chambersburg PA
CBHW081405170526
45166CB00010B/3208